Musings

of a

Gray Flannel
Tramp

Written By
MAURICE K. ISAAC

Illustrated By
MATTHEW E. ISAAC

Published by Eye of Infinity.
Printed by Lulu Press, Inc.

ISBN: 978-0-615-93656-7

First Printing.

Musings

of a

Gray Flannel Tramp

Written By
Maurice K. Isaac

Illustrated By
Matthew E. Isaac

EYE OF INFINITY

Dedicate to

Tamara
who
got me started,

and

Ann
who
kept me going.

Contents

Foreword

The title of this volume is a reference to the dichotomy between my childhood ambition to be a tramp, based on reading "The Road" by Jack London and "Autobiography of a Super-Tramp" by W. H. Davies, and the mundane reality of life as a geophysicist. It is also a recognition that much of my inspiration comes to me on solitary walks.

As far as the arts are concerned, I have always respected industry, form and discipline, preferring baroque to romantic music, and representational art to the moderns. I believe that, geniuses and idiot savants aside, the best work is produced by journeymen who learn their trade through long years of discipline, sweat and toil.

Since I came to writing late in life, and did not have years to study, I settled for the discipline of form. I try, to the best of my ability, to write lines that scan and rhyme. I read all the great English poets, and borrow shamelessly. However, while it is not too difficult, given time and energy, to write, for example, a sonnet that is perfect as to its rhymes and iambic pentameters, the real problem is "inspiration". What should one write about?

I quickly found, if I wanted to be convincing and interesting, it was best to write about people I knew, autobiographical incidents, pet peeves, or the odd thoughts that crossed my mind during my daily walks around the block. Most of the poems in this small volume fall into one of those categories. The exceptions are historical works, and paeans to the variety and beauty of the English language.

I have not pulled any punches. I write what I feel, and I am sure that very few could read this volume and not be offended by one or more poems. However, it is my hope that everyone will be able to identify with some of my thoughts and feelings, and perhaps gain some new perspectives and insights into commonplace situations, objects and ideas. Above all I want to entertain. If you read this volume without once cracking a smile, or pumping your fist, or swearing at me, I will have failed.

Maurice K. Isaac
Houston
December 2013

Musings
of a
Gray Flannel Tramp

In Praise of English as the Language of Poetry

When wishing to communicate
A new or subtle message
It's always good to contemplate
The vagaries of verbiage

It isn't strange the Eskimo
Who lives where it's ubiquitous
Should have so many words for snow
Just makes him sound meticulous

But why should those who always praise
All forms of automation
Have quite so many different ways
To talk of ambulation

If nature's wonders we would taste
We hike or trek, or ramble
But if we've lots of time to waste
We saunter, stroll or amble

When we're well dressed and confident
We prance and strut our stuff
But if we're poor and diffident
Then shuffle, shamble, scuff

The soldiers who defend our land
Parade, patrol and march in step,
But hobos, on the other hand,
Will wander, tramp and schlep

In Aussie they "go walkabout"
To get their heads together
While Brits just "hit the road" and shout
About the awful weather   .

The poor will ride on "Shank's mare"
The rich may promenade
So some will say that is not fair
And start a new crusade

But I will give a hearty thanks
To former occupiers
Whose tongues have helped to swell the ranks
Of English versifiers

"Definitely" Random Quotes

I had a dream the other day
I wrote a plagiarizing lay
That used no words that were my own
Just blooms by English poets grown
And, though it rhymed, it did not scan
With nonsense all my verses ran
An unconnected word collage
A mad poetical mirage

"To be or not to be that is
My last Duchess painted on the wall
A still unravished bride of quietness
A cry of nations o'er thy sunken halls

Absent from thee I languish still
For never yet was honest man
Amid a host of Golden Daffodils
In Xanadu with Kubla Khan

There's a breathless hush in the close tonight
The curfew tolls the knell of parting day
Ere long they come where that same wicked wight
Said gather ye rosebuds while ye may

On Wenlock edge the wood's in trouble
"Just the place for a Snark!" the Bellman cried
Double, double toil and trouble
Announced by all the trumpets of the sky

Wake! For the sun who scattered into Flight
Busie old foole, unruly sunne
A Tyger, Tyger burning bright
If you make a revolution, make it for fun"

Perhaps sophisticated minds
Might search my lines some sense to find
As critics have a wont to do
And my poor efforts misconstrue
Deduce a meaning all their own
Suck blood from unresponsive stone
Report that I must be inspired
And as a genius be admired
For writing such amazing stuff
But then I'd have to cry "enough!"
I merely thumb anthologies
And jumble lines just how I please
No thought of sense but only rhyme
An exercise to pass the time

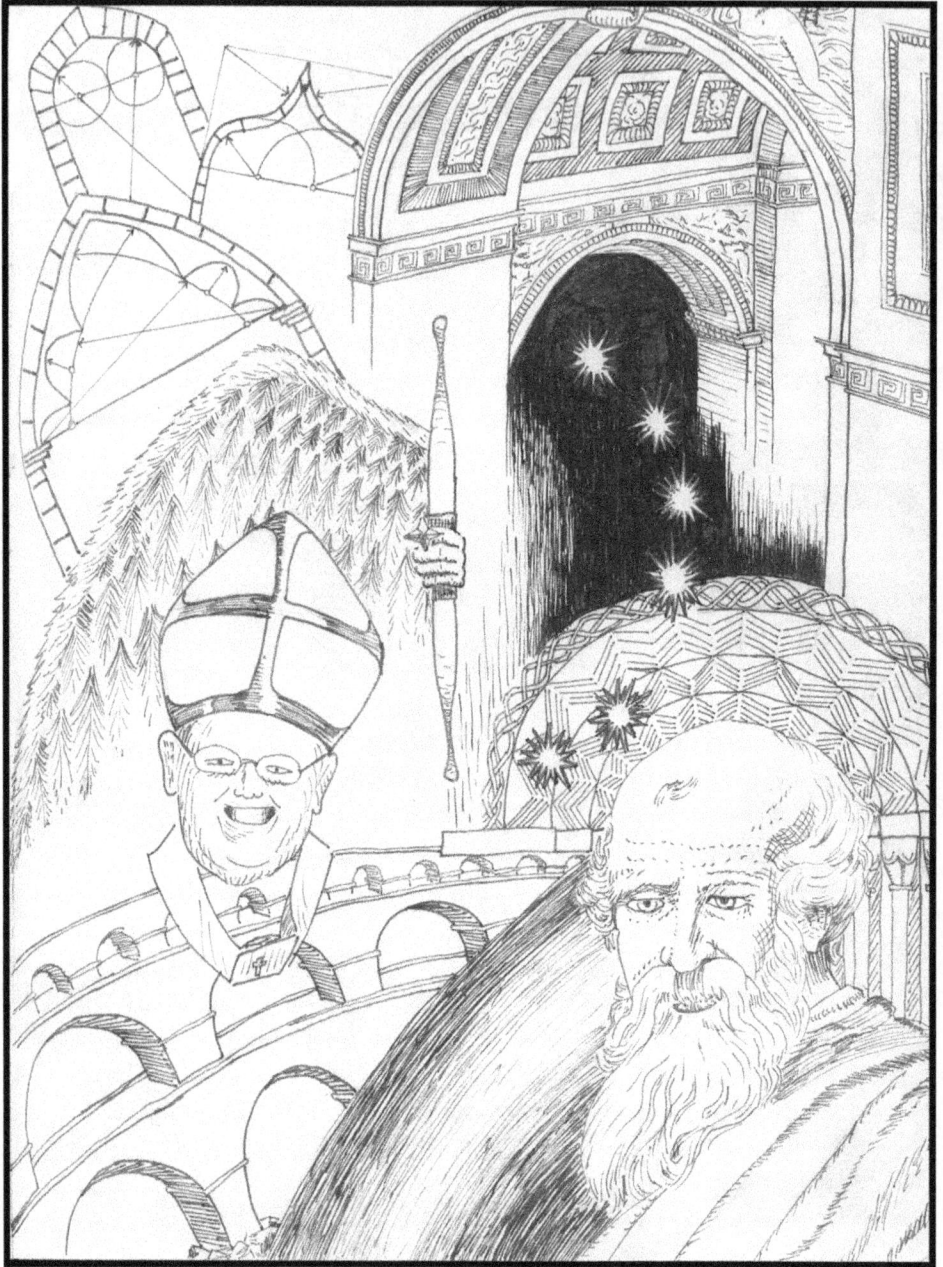

Archly Arches

Orion's starry bow, across the heaven
Awakes my sleeping muse to thoughts
Of arches, arcs and famous men
Whose architectural genius sought
To capture nature's forms, and so to bend
Their beauty by an iron will,
Man's structural oeuvres might transcend
The works of God, and yet fulfill
An act of homage to their Lord

Norman and Gothic arches, brick and stone
Supporting bridges, aqueducts, cathedrals
Churches, abbeys, and those overblown
Triumphal gates, that later mark the fall
Of short lived conquerors, overthrown
By newer, crueler, and more potent lives.
Their evanescent temporal fame outgrown
While builders stand immortalized
By constructs of the trowel not the sword

Then thoughts to arch as prefix stray
What power to every office it can add
Archbishop, angel, duke, they all may say
I have more influence when clad
In titles arch, than in my costliest array
Of vestments, uniforms, or myriad
Medals, ribbons, even fine display
Of polished armor ironclad.
An arch to every office insolence affords

Or arch as bow, as archery
A skill by England's yeomen used
To thrice deflower French chivalry
Humiliated, beaten and abused.
Or rain arch, bow, God's promise plain
That never will he flood the earth again
Despite our actions inhumane
And evil works done in his name.
However much they are deplored

And finally the arch in famous names
Plutarch, Petrarch, and Archimedes, who
With teacher Archie Preston, I must blame
For love of Romans, poems, wars and screws.
But now I archly must confess
The muse has left me in distress
My best upon this subject I've expressed
And am no longer by the arch obsessed
So leave all other archways unexplored

The Chorister

He's eager to raise his voice to God's glory
In thanks for all blessings received
And spread the good news of the wonderful story
To those who have yet to believe

Alas, as he waits to sing the first hymn
Process down the aisle to the altar
He's mostly concerned not to damage a limb
Or to hurry or stumble or falter

Safe in the stalls he sings out with great verve
But then, as he sits down to pray
Instead of just listening he starts to observe
Just who will be singing today

He stands for the lesson and follows along
Counting the errors in diction
And thinks what a pity it just sounds so wrong
He'd read it with much more conviction

The sermon is long which gives him a chance
To count all the lights in the ceiling
Then slowly drift off in a somnolent trance
Thank God he is sitting not kneeling

With a final amen the sermon has ended
Now it is time for the creed
His reading is perfect his diction is splendid
God suffered for all our misdeeds

The moment has come he rises to utter
The glorious offertory anthem
Tallis or Purcell or only John Rutter
He prays it brings in a king's ransom

The choir sings on as Communion is taken
Then down to partake they're all sent
Except for a few whose credos unshaken
Still force them to show their dissent

At last it is over and all that remains
Is marching once more down the aisle
By saving his voice he can sing the last strains
And is able to end with a smile

The Birdwatcher

When he retired in one-nine-nine-nine,
He thought he had plenty to do,
But his wife whispered "Honey, dear heart of mine,
Have I got a hobby for you!

I know you love rivers, and mountains and trees,
And hiking, no matter the weather.
Why don't you watch birds, I hear it's a breeze,
What's more we can do it together."

They purchased some field glasses, strong for old eyes,
The best bird books money could buy.
Set off for the mountains and wide open skies,
Some rare birds to identify.

They drove to Big Bend, and there, on a lake,
Dabbling and diving, espied
Some plain, duck like birds, the color of slate.
"Let's see what they are", his wife cried.

Out came the bird guide, with pictures quite clear,
But none seemed just right for their ducks.
He thumbed through the book, and said with a sneer,
"I knew it, this bird watching sucks".

His wife, more persistent, cried "lets not give in!"
Through the pages continued to root.
Then said, with a very superior grin,
"Its just an American Coot."

The Party

Last Sunday was a very busy day
With bags of bottles, butts, and food, decayed,
Tossed in a dumpster half a block away.
The sheets were washed, and every bed remade.
The carpets vacuumed, and the rug was moved
To hide the blood red stain of who knows what.
The dishes shone, so none could disapprove.
Even the patio was not forgot.
So when that night our errant parents found
Us watching noisy movies in the den,
They were so pleased, to find all safe and sound,
They happily went off to bed, but then
Next day, our father very sternly said
"Whose are those panties underneath our bed"

Inspired by family reminiscences around the table
at Christmas 2012

Houston Floods

There are no hills in Houston town
So when the rain comes pouring down
From tropic storm or hurricane
It never roars across the plain
Or sweeps our precious cars away
Down Buffalo Bayou to the bay

And yet it quickly fills each ditch
Floods street and underpass, the which
Plays havoc with the traffic flow.
Then every car is stuck on slow
And many stall and block the way
So tempers rise and nerves may fray

To fund an anti flood crusade
The citizens a tax have paid
For dams and sewers, to contain
The flow of water to the main,
And keep their houses and their streets
In safety, till the flood retreats

A horseshoe levy to the west
Holds back the bayou waters lest
They rise to block the sewer flow
That drains the city, and thus slow
The dropping level in the street
And complex drainage plans defeat

Lay Houston's sewers out to see
And they would stretch from sea to sea
But none can view this mighty work
For underneath the ground it lurks
Dark, silent, empty, when its dry,
But dangerous when the heavens cry

But as I make my morning round
My eyes are cast down to the ground
And so I see, as most do not,
Or, if they do, don't give a jot,
The iron eyelids over all
The windows to the sewer's soul

One hundred twenty thousand holes
Ingress and egress do control
To subterranean pipes that send
The excess water to its end
Where bayous meet the cleansing bay
And flush our petty sins away

From whence do all these covers come
An iron masterpiece each one
With patterns and designs to praise
Their maker, or a catchy phrase
As pelican and fish give voice
"Clean water" is our "Clear choice"

East Jordan Iron works can claim
The most, but close behind it's plain
Is India. But who could think
It economical to sink
Such capital into a hole
Only flood victims might extol

Into my mind suspicions leap
It cannot be so very cheap
To ship cast iron from foreign shores
Oh how my parsimonious heart deplores
Such wanton government excess
I feel my views I must express

But then, the price is not germane
For those in need will not complain,
Lest drains are blocked and waters rise
Insurance claims rise to the skies
And all their property is lost
Then all that matters is their cost.

Morning Walk

Though solitary, my morning walk resounds
With neighbors greetings and the friendly sounds
Of garbage men, who wave from two wheeled bins
And speed from house to house to hide the sins
Of gluttony, addiction and excess,
Amid compacted mounds of household mess

The merry bands of ethnic mowers stop,
And check me out, as if I were a cop,
Who might their immigration status check
And dreams of fiscal independence wreck,
Or are they just exceedingly well trained
And wish to keep my walking clothes unstained

Construction work is governed by the clock
And, though new houses rise on every block,
The sawing hammering and the staple gun
Are silent till the rising of the sun
So early workers, often full of smiles
Will wave as I pound out my morning miles

The cleaner, babysitter and housemaid
I see arrive by bus to ply their trade
In self imposed domestic slavery
To keep their families, not in luxury,
But better far than in their homes of old
Before they moved where streets are paved with gold

And lastly, all those dogs I can't abide,
As they approach, I always move aside
To pass the owner, not the dog, since he,
Or, much more often, she, will surely be
Much less inclined to bark, or sniff my crotch,
And so I safely end my morning watch

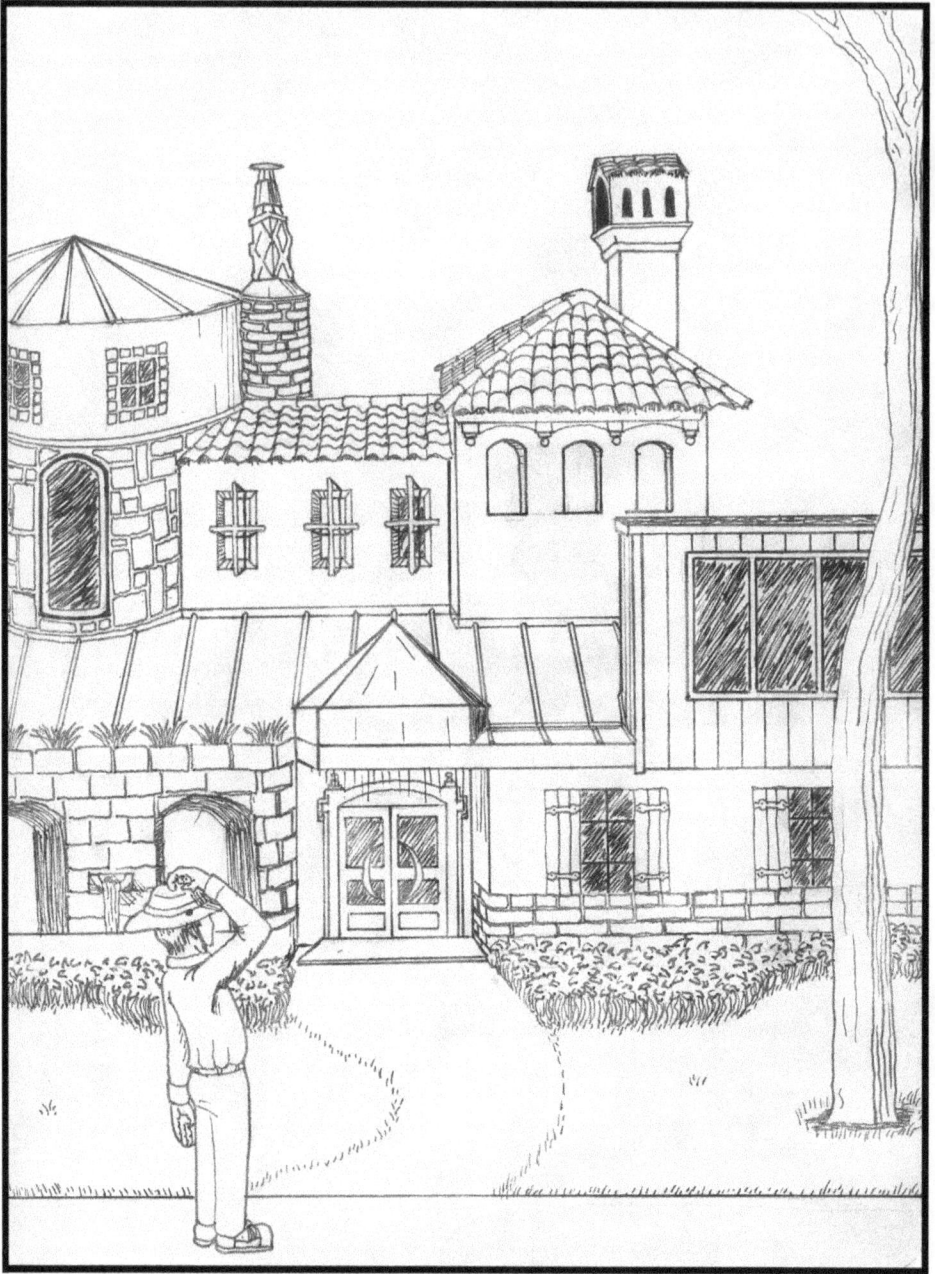

Houston Houses

Why do these mansions so offend my eyes
Replete with architectural excess
Odd chimneys, columns, bell less towers arise
Roofs tiled, metaled, pitched or pitch-less
Find support from brick or stucco, stone,
Or honest wood, that is the skeleton
Of every private home within this zone
Where not a soul can bear to be out done
Fueled by an over powering drive, that cares
No whit for beauty, harmony or place
But how this symbol of their wealth compares
To that of other souls, alas misplaced
From old traditions that might yet embrace
The disciplines of structure form and taste

Memorial Mall

A walk around Memorial Mall
Must be conducted at a crawl
And only rain and thunder storm
Can make me brave the teeming swarm
Of huddled masses, now set free,
To slouch and shop and hinder me.
Ill dressed ill kempt and out of shape,
They make me long for quick escape
Back to the lighting, wind and rain,
But then a voice says, "No! Remain"
And ask them if they ever think,
While guzzling sugar loaded drink,
And hamburgers and greasy fries
About events "Memorialized"
By Houston's famous road and park,

Or are their lives without a spark
Of civic interest or pride,
Content in ignorance to ride
Upon the backs of those who stood
And fought for freedom and the good
In world wide struggles long ago
Against a European foe

But fearful of a rude reply
I stumble onward as I try
To find a sympathetic face
No matter what its creed or race
Which might an honest answer give
And such a questioner forgive

But suddenly to my surprise
I hear, unquestioned, these replies
Where modest storefronts advertise
These simple patriotic cries
We're Army, Navy and Marines
Join us and we will give you means
To serve your country and inspire
A love of honor and desire
To be the best that you can be
And learn a little history

The storm clouds part the sun comes out
I leave the mall and never doubt
That fitness, honor, history
 Are staples of our military

The End of Books?

My house is jammed with books of every size
Shelves bookcases and closets double stacked
At least two thousand volumes, which comprise
A library that I would keep intact
Not just for now, but for posterity
A foolish self indulgent vanity

But though I love these books, I feel oppressed
I live in fear of book worms, fire and flood
Possessing them and yet by them possessed
I feel I should defend them with my blood
Displayed and catalogued with awful care
In cases costly, elegant and rare

I'm told that my salvation lies in E
E-libraries E-books E-everything
Then all my books and many more, could be
Contained within the compass of a thing
No bigger than the merest novelette
Or stored in clouds within the internet

Yet all my years of reading make me feel
An electronic book does not exist
A book is not ethereal, but real
A solid artifact that must consist
Of ink imprinted pages tightly bound
With solid boards dust jacketed around

And what if every blessed book was E
No need for printers, bookstores, libraries
For all could search their little screens and see
A thousand times a thousand books, and seize
Whatever caught their fancy, and download
So they might read in bed or on the road

So many simple joys would disappear
No leather bindings, bookplates, sneaky peak
To check friends' books, and no more chance to hear
Those well know desert island Crusoes speak
Of books that for their exile they would pack
Why choose just one when you can take a MAC

And books would be just artifacts in dusty
Antiquarian shops, with records, tapes and
Laser discs. Detritus of a musty
Age, when everything was done by hand
But what will happen when the power runs out!!
Then I will laugh and cry and boldly shout!!
COME READ MY NON E-BOOKS AND WEEP

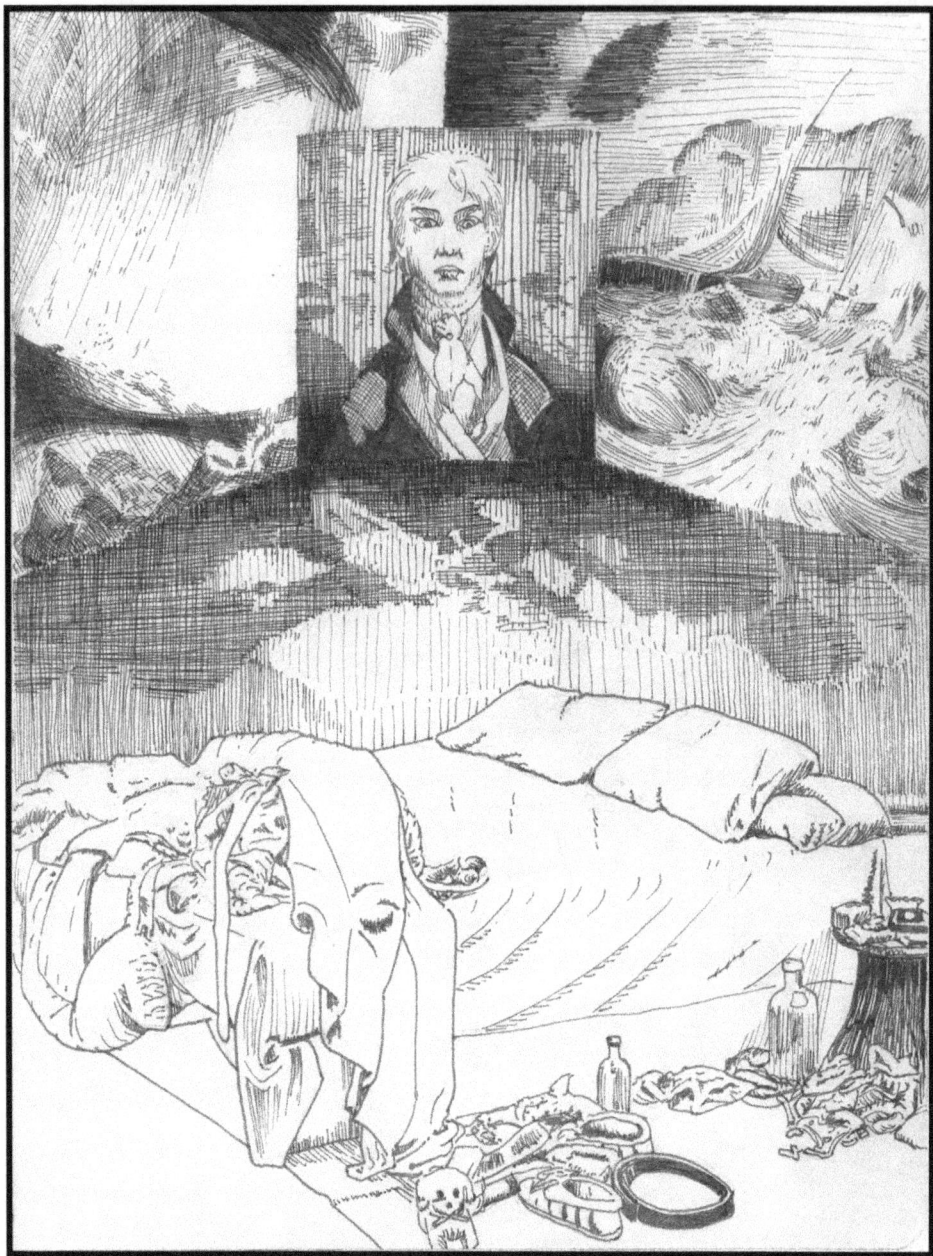

On Tracey Emin Being Considered for the Turner Prize

So, what would Joseph Mallord William Turner think
Of that crass, undeserved, prize, now given,
In his name, for works, whose coarseness shrinks
Delight in art that, by inspired craftsmen,
At the peak of hard won expertise,
Might move our souls to an uplifted sense
Of beauty, and not kowtow to journalese,
Assaulting by its cant our commonsense,
That tells us soiled panties, condoms, and
Detritus of an ill spent night, are not
An inspiration we can understand,
But rather something we should all boycott.
"Though they have found a thing more black than black
Were I to use it as they do, I'd be a hack"

Lost

With satellites and other gear
This modern age has banished fear
There's no excuse for being lost
For at a very modest cost
Your GPS can find the way
And you need never go astray

Yet some, at such devices sneer
Who've felt that shivery touch of fear
On lonely walks across the moor,
When sun dips down and mists obscure
A path that once had seemed so clear
But now begins to disappear

It's when you know you must depend
On compass, map and wit to bend
And to advantage use that fear
To find your way on paths unclear
A touch of danger thrills your sense
Makes every feeling more intense

Though I've been lost three times before
In snow, on mountain and on moor
Yet I would lose myself again
In any sort of wild terrain
If once more I might just contrive
To feel so totally alive

Doctor, Doctor!

Time was, I thought that Doctors' words were law
Until I learned, they too have feet of straw
Are subject to the same impediments
To health and wealth, life's cruel discontents,
That plague the rest of us, who have not sworn
The Hippocratic oath, and do not scorn
Pursuit of profit from our customers
Who to our hard won expertise defer

Thanks to the government, they're often bound
By protocols that call for tests unbound
By any diagnostic skill, or cost
But are designed to limit any loss
From lawsuits brought by friend or relative
That ultra liberal courts might not forgive
Imposing huge, unconscionable, fines
Which real sufferers' care can undermine

They test our blood, and then they test again
Despite our protests that we feel no pain
To gauge how far from their "perfection"
We have strayed, and then attempt correction
To an imaginary, ideal norm
No man or woman fit since they were born
Till every visit makes us feel depressed
And with our failing health we are obsessed

Then, to be safe, they are conservative,
Dispensing pills, that we might never live
With aches and pains that are a natural part
Of growing old, as circulation, joints and heart
Harden and clog, with age and time's decay
So we might never tempted be to say
Why can't they make me feel just as I was
When sight and sound and smell were all abuzz

Yet, as a realist, I'm proud to say
That swallowing prescriptions every day
To make me feel that I am twenty-five
Is not the way I want to stay alive
I'd rather eat and drink just what I please
Run, walk, and exercise, or take my ease
I'd rather suffer cruel times decay
Take my genetic chances come what may

Two Lions

To cap a week of walking in Big Bend
On our last day, we visited a waterhole
To see the sunrise, and perhaps to spend
A happy hour birding, and to stroll
Among the bushes and the cottonwoods

As on our tip toes we approached the pond,
Me leading, Jim a pace or two behind,
He softly whispered, "look, but don't respond.
I think, except for birds, you must be blind.
You passed a lion sitting in that tree"

I turned, and with astonishment beheld
Not just a single lion, but a pair,
Just ten yards off, so close I could have smelled
Them, had I senses half so fine as theirs,
Lolling together on a leafy branch.

The thought that visitors so seldom see
Puma concolor in their natural habitat,
Quite overwhelmed our caution, so that we,
In silence, watched these beautiful, yet lethal, cats
And threw all thoughts of safety to the wind.

One sat, the other lay, sideways turning,
Dark silhouettes against the rising sun.
Silent, unmoving, eyes brightly burning
Stared back at us unblinking. Should we run,
The car was far away parked on the road.

And yet, as we looked closely at the pair,
They seemed quite safe, and small and, all unwary,
Shared an odd companionable air,
Like siblings, but without the rivalry.
Two juveniles without a lioness.

We watched and photographed until, at last,
They turned, and dropping silently to earth,
Fast disappeared, the magic moment past,
And we were left to ponder on the dearth,
In city life, of such uplifting sights.

Mourning Doves and Passenger Pigeons

The family Columbidae is dear
To those who worship harmony and peace
With olive branch they send a message clear
The hope that war and violence will decrease.
Yet godless men with traps and guns once crushed
This symbolism by a heinous crime
Of avian genocide that must disgust
All ornithologists who have the time
To mourn the passing of Ectopistes.
A genus so prolific and widespread
It's flock wings beating caused a gentle breeze
And, for a moment, made a shadow overhead.
Still, others of the family mourn their kin
With spotted plumage, whitterings and coos
And seem forgiving of the mortal sin
That caused their gentle brethren to lose
Their place in nature's cruel hierarchy

On Walking
the SW Coast Path

Walking south, the sea's on my right hand,
From cliff top far below, from beach quite near.
Across the wrack, feeding upon the land,
Interminably grinding year on year,
Rocks into pebbles, shingle, sand, silt,
Swept from the coast to settle in the deep,
To be compressed once more to rock, then built,
Into new towering cliffs, jagged, steep,
But my concern is with my aching legs.
Tired by uneven step and steep incline,
My mind dwells on the nearest pub, where kegs
Of cold lager, beer or wine, will realign
My thoughts in channels much more practical,
And banish any musings geological.

Thoughts on Visiting Hadrian's Wall

We leave the bus and climb a gravel way,
Through noisy sheep, and dark depressing rain.
Mere remnants of the wall in Hadrian's day,
From centuries of harsh neglect remain.
We stand where Romans scanned the hills for Picts,
And dream of other countries, other walls,
Built with the harsh intention to restrict
Invaders, or escapees from their thrall,
And wonder if the building of a wall
Is but precursor to an Empire's fall.
Though Babylon, and China's walls remain,
The dynasties that built them do not reign.
So, what of Texas, and our southern fence
Salvation, or a hopeless doomed defense.

Battle of Britain

The Poles, whose charge saved Christendom, before Vienna's
walls,
Have charged again, alas in vain, against the Nazi hordes.
The British ultimatum has expired with no withdrawals.
The Allies have unsheathed their rusty swords.

The ogre in the Kremlin has been slavering at the feast
Of little Baltic nations, he might stuff into his craw.
So, by blackmail, tricks, deceit, and violence, he increased
The pressure, till he's gobbled up them all.

The forces of the Empire will be heeding Britain's call,
But threats from closer foes, make them look to their defense,
And uncommitted countries wait to see where chips may fall,
While across the sea the "States" sit on the fence.

The French and Dutch and Belgians have been blitzkrieged
to defeat,
While the British Expedition, once trapped on Dunkirk beach,
Thanks to Herculean efforts and self-sacrificing feats,
In impotence retreats from German reach.

As Nazi boots are crushing the Elysian fields of France,
The Fuehrer, in his eagle's nest, sits planning the demise
Of that lonely little island, that blocks his next advance,
But not until the Luftwaffe rules the skies.

Since William conquered England, she has never been enslaved
No foreign power or alien fleet could pierce Britannia's shield,
For British ships, and British men, for eons ruled the waves,
But can her sons an aerial buckler wield.

Now Goering promised Hitler that, in just a few short weeks,
His Messerschmidts and Heinkels would force Britain to
concede.
Would clear her skies of fighters, and a dreadful havoc wreak.
Destroy her airfields and her pilots bleed.

But, as flights of Nazi eagles drone westward to their prey,
Bold, radar guided, dragon swarms spit fire from every side,
To scatter, burn and decimate, imperial display,
Force Nazi dreams of victory to subside.

Then, by ill fated accident, or heavenly design,
Bombs drop on central London, thus arousing Winston's ire,
And to toughen the resistance, and put steel in Britain's spine,
The city of Berlin is set on fire.

This so incenses Hitler, that he orders his attacks
To leave beleaguered airfields, and to bomb the cities flat,
Which gives the RAF time to regroup, and plug the cracks,
And send new planes and pilots into bat.

Now aerial attrition starts to swing Great Britain's way.
Though Germans rain down fire and death, on factory and
town,
The heavy price, in men and planes, is more than they can pay
So invasion plans are canceled, the battle has been won.

Inspired by Galileo's Last Words

"Eppur si muove", is the cry, of those,
Whose honest scientific souls demand,
They tell the emperor when he has no clothes,
And all the evil consequence withstand.
Thank God no Spanish Inquisition rules,
To tell us what we may or may not think,
But groups of pseudo scientific fools,
With malice, still exaggerate the link
Between a small, and possibly benign,
Adjustment of the global temperatures,
And increase in a gas which, by design,
The health of every verdant plant ensures.
So let us all with Galileo shout,
Do not the scientific method flout

Governmental Hubris

There always is a tendency
For those in the ascendancy
To get a bit above themselves
And say,

We know that you've elected us,
But if you give us too much fuss,
Your cross, and car, and gun, we'll take
Away

Since they are far too dangerous
To life and limb, and also us,
For you to keep for even one
More day.

The way to solve our fiscal mess,
Is tax and penalize success,
And make the idle rich their fair
Share pay.

As for talk radio and FOX,
We'll put them in a sound proof box,
Bury it deep and throw the key
Away.

Because we don't like CO2,
We'll force, with regulations new,
Those dirty coal fired plants to
Over pay.

So what if that means, sometime soon,
You suffer blackouts, and consume
A box of candles every single
Day.

Good health and safety is our goal,
So we intend to tell you all
Just what to eat and drink, and how
To play.

We feel we are responsible
To keep you from whatever ill,
The awful risks of life may throw
Your way.

And since we feel you're pretty dumb,
And may to blandishments succumb,
We plan to take the internet
Away.

This attitude so arrogant,
Just makes me want to scream and rant,
And to the proud majority
Convey

A prayer, that the electorate,
Whom you with hubris have beset,
Will in November vote to end
Your stay.

Discretion

Its not so very long ago
That wires connected every phone.
Ma Bell the only way to go
To talk to others from your home.

You'd wind the handle to alert
An operator to connect,
But then, discretion you'd exert,
Your "private" business to protect.

You'd think with care just what to say,
Because you knew another ear,
With accidental malice, may
Your dearest secrets overhear.

Now, stupidly, we oft assume
That no one hears just what we say.
Yet unknown forces plot our doom,
Record the errors of each day.

Now we're in touch by internet,
With e-mail, voice, and simple text
Its all too easy to suspect
Each word, if judged without context.

Now I might say "Obama's great,
His policies I know will make
An end to malice, envy, hate"
But what might a computer take?

"Obama's policies I hate"
And so condemn me, context less,
A dangerous enemy of state.
Oh what an undeserved mess!

The moral of this story is,
Be careful what you write or say,
And keep your confidential biz
As far from other ears you may.

Sequestration

So times are hard, you're out of work,
Your bills are driving you berserk.
What can you do to make all right.
To save your credit and, despite
A lack of income, still provide
Food, shelter, and so keep your pride,
And stay as happy as a lark.

We know it's difficult to choose
Just what must go, what you will lose.
So, why not look to government,
Which constantly has overspent
Its income, and at last must cut
"Essential" services and start to shut
The libraries and National Parks.

As warring parties could not reach
Agreement, as to just how each
Department might reduce it's call
Upon the resource that we all
Reluctantly with tax supply.
Then sequestration was the cry.
We'll cut just like a great white shark.

No finesse, merely randomly.
We'll trim the fat, then oversee
Reduction of the body whole.
Maximum pain will be our goal.
To teach a lesson hard to those,
Who think that government should close,
And set itself a new benchmark.

So, in our private lives, should we
Cut mortgage payments, oversee
Reductions in our credit score,
From unpaid statements we ignore.
Pretend the company that keeps us warm,
By going green will now transform
Into a kindly matriarch.

Who doesn't care if payment's late,
Because the Feds remunerate
All honest efforts, which include
Commitment to a resolution crude;
No oil, no gas, no coal or wood,
But energy, that for our good,
Leaves no environmental mark.

Then, as to food, we know it's good
To cut those calories that could
Increase our chance of getting fat.
But surely God made bacon, that
We might the taste of Brussels sprouts
Endure. So do not go without
Your pork. It always hits the mark.

And never fear if you get sick,
Unless your old, then please die quick.
Since money's short, we'll have to give
Priority to those who've lived
An alcohol and smoke free life.
Thin as a rake with just one wife,
With purity to rival Joan of Arc.

So Government will lead the way,
And to our children we can say,
We followed where Obama led,
We listened to just what he said,
And now we are far up the creek.
Our sad economy is Greek.
The future of the USA is bleak.

Loo Lines

As opera lovers we confess
Listening to Wagner creates stress
Interminable hours in our seat
Brief intermissions to excrete
The food and drink that we imbibe
To help our harried minds transcribe
German *Angst* to English, Russian
French, Chinese or Italian
That we might understand the sense
Of stories, so arcane and dense
Created by a mastermind
Whose every thought was unconfined
Requiring effort so profound
His subtle meanings to propound

And then, between the acts, we are,
By calls of nature cruel and bizarre
Subjected to a torture so
Grotesque, that trudging round we go
Like prisoners long in durance pent
Now exercising with intent,
In "LOO" lines, shuffling and slow
Exchanging comforting "bon mot"
How it is better to be slow
Than operations undergo.
Until, at last, we reach the end
Relieved, with confidence ascend
The stairway to the second act
To once again with genius interact

The Thin Red Line

We know each generation will bestow
New meanings on evocative bon mot.
For some **"the thin red line"** evokes
A powerful image that uncloaks
Forgotten memories of Victorian war.
Unmoving highlanders who underscore
The power of simultaneous discharge.
Crimea, Alma, and the "charge"
Yet opera buffs may say, the true red line
Is drawn by heavenly design
Around the throat of blessed Marguerite,
Whose goodness Hell could not defeat,
Or lovers of the twentieth century,
May think of Wozzeck's murder of Marie,
And thank the lord that crimson necklaces
Are not a part of modern dress,
But those who study music history know,
That were it not for Guido Monaco's
Red line, to help his choir boys incant,
We'd have no music but Gregorian chant

Sexual Ambivalence
Girls As Boys

Today, the blatant sexuality
Of pelvic pumping divas by the score,
Offends my native sensibility,
Though you may think my prudishness a bore.

I turn for subtler ambiguity,
To gender bending operatic roles.
Where girls play boys, with sensitivity
That moves an old man's sentimental soul.

Octavian, Oskar, Cherubino all,
By mezzos, full of boyish charms, are sung.
Their youthful beauty holds me in its thrall,
By them my rusty bell of lust is rung.

So my advice to maidens, who would meet
An educated and a well bred man,
A little bit of AC/DC, but discrete,
And pretty soon you'll have him in the can.

On Revisiting San Francisco

The city by the bay has lost her way,
And like an aging courtesan she hides
The harsh and cruel signs of time's decay,
With paint and plaster covering her sides.

The cable cars with tourists over-filled,
Efficiently, by large wise-cracking men,
Still clang and claw their way from hill to hill.
The views of Bay and Bridge still rate a ten.

Yet she looks fairer far from distant heights,
Than on her traffic clogged and dirty streets,
Side walks defiled by sad un-cared for wights,
Who all attempts at cleanliness defeat.

Encouraged, by a liberal policy
Of laissez faire, to sleep upon the street,
Bundled in doorways, for the world to see,
They prick the conscience of a rich elite.

To leave the opera house and take the tram
Down smelly Market street to welcome Powell,
Avoid the sleepers, make pan handlers scram,
Engenders a desire to scream and howl,

Oh God there has to be a better way
To run a city, once so far apart,
So new, bedazzled, visitors still say,
That San Francisco's where they left their heart.

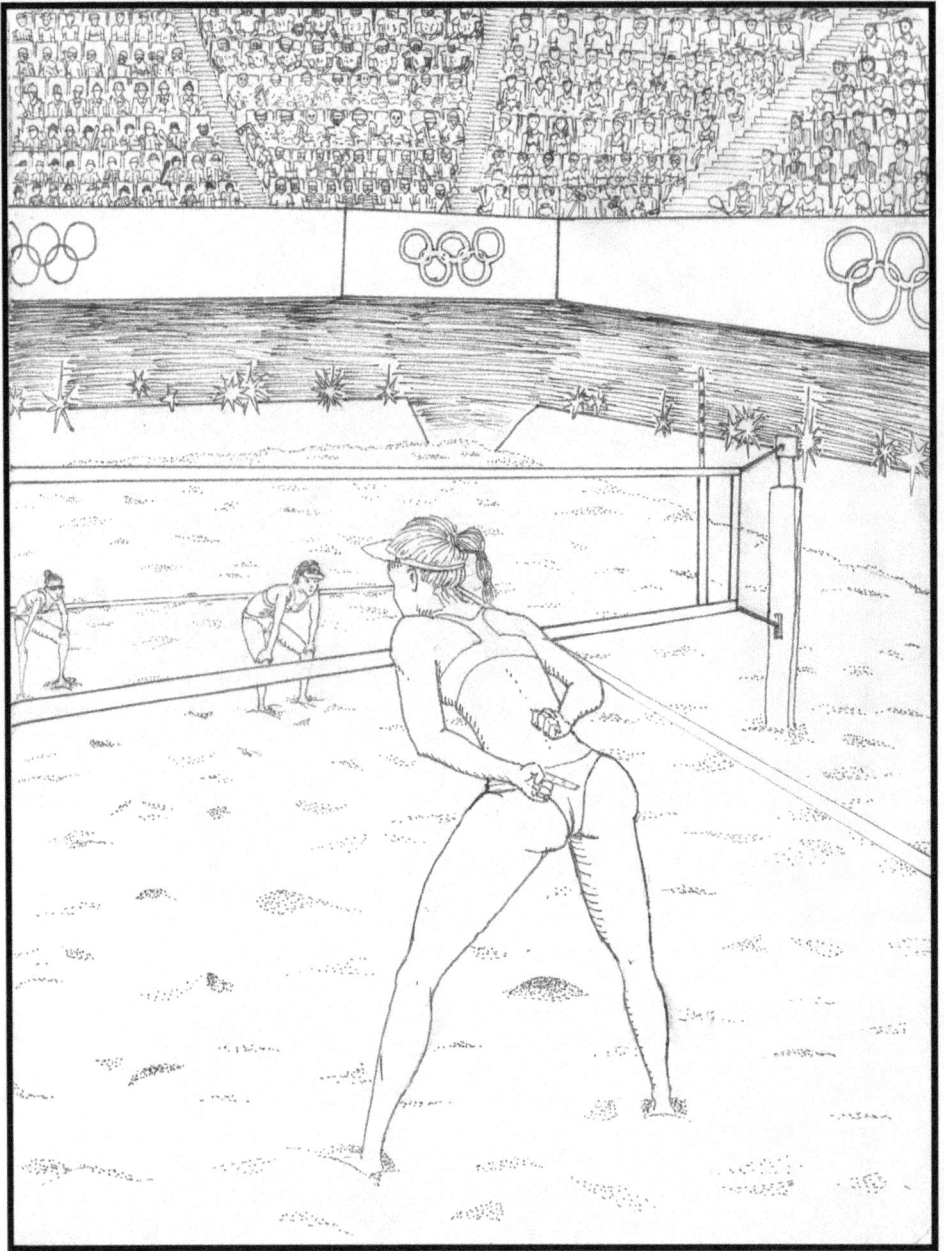

World Champion

Who'd not aspire to be world champion
Train, sacrifice and stake your all upon
A sporting trial, and winning it, inflame
Its loyal fans, to make your name
A household tweet, on every cell.
So famous, with it you might sell
Ice cream to Eskimos, honey to bees,
And talk and act just how you please.

But just what contest should you choose,
To pique the fans and make the news?
No pucks, or stones on ice rinks curdled,
Or endless jumps by horses hurdled.
No running, either fast or long,
Or throwing things that land just wrong,
Or jumping obstacles or pits,
Or sports where you must count the hits.

No games which from their origins have strayed,
And by commercial changes so decayed,
That only in one country they are played,
Where "World" championships are just charade.
Or games that only can be fought
On courts and courses just the rich support.
Or, rarer yet, those games whose greatest worth,
Stems from the English schools that gave them birth.

Or games, so governed by "the clock"
That, in the final moments, players mock
The rules, and by deliberately fouling,
Seconds of critical advantage wring.
Where disregard of sportsmanship
Is sanctioned, and approved as hip,
By referees and fans alike,
Yet fills me with intense dislike.

No contests which for safety's sake require
A certain type of bodily attire,
Support for those, whose powerful physique
Intimidates us, so we dare not speak,
The undeniable sartorial truth
A six inch belt is just uncouth.
No matter what you snatch or press,
Our sensibilities you'll not impress.

No sport that for its outcome must depend
On biased judges, who may recommend
Contestants who are clearly not the best,
But know some bureaucratic pest,
Who helps them on their undeserved way
To fame and fortune, so they may repay
The favor by a future quid pro quo,
When from the final podium they go.

No games that are so loved by all,
They have too many heroes to recall,
Or races that defy the naked eye
To choose the winner, and rely
On complicated timers to resolve
Hundredths of seconds, and absolve
Judges from all responsibility,
With total electronic credibility.

No sport that, for its greatest thrills,
Depends on prepubescent girls,
Or wonderfully muscled youths,
Whose acrobatic feats, forsooth,
Exhibit disregard for life and limb,
That in another context would seem grim.
Or schools of mermaids who must swim
In tight formations. Oh so prim!

No sport it is impossible to win
Without succumbing to a venial sin,
And cheating, by illegal use
Of substances, whose goal is to produce
Performances that utterly destroy
Those who no esoteric drugs employ.
Blameless competitors who have no chance
In any competition held in France.

No sport that uses artificial aids
Like wheels or sleds or skis or blades,
To increase mans mobility or speed,
For then the competition starts to feed
On innovations in design,
Rather than prowess of the frame divine.
Till finally committees must decide
How long and hard and smooth and wide.

No headless goats by wild riders born,
No games where armor must be worn,
No guns or bows or rapiers,
Or even hammers shots or spears.
No bats or clubs, lacrosse or hockey sticks,
Or any sporting weapon, that inflicts
Bodily harm on those who play the game.
Who wants their blood to be the price of fame?

No, I would choose a newer game,
That offers health and wealth and fame,
That can be played in every country that
Has deserts, beaches, or a sandy flat.
That is so simple anyone can play,
As long as they've a body to display,
That's long and lean and minus any fat.
"Beach Volley Ball" is where it's at!

To Bethany Hamilton
Soul Surfer

Some years ago I went to stay
At Kauai's Hanalei,
Where Puff the Magic Dragon lay
And frolicked harmlessly.

And there, alas, I must confess,
I was embarrassed sore,
When by a click I gave distress
To one I now adore.

At sunset's hour I walked with friends
On Hanalei's pier,
And there within my camera's lens
The sunset did appear.

Quick as a flash I took the shot,
But much to my dismay,
Bethany and friend were who I caught,
Alas, what could I say.

In silhouette for all to see
Her missing arm was clear,
As was her anger equally,
Which pierced me like a spear.

She thought that I, with ghoulish joy,
A paparazzi bold,
My evil camera did employ
To garner pots of gold.

So I kept mum, said not a word,
And thought what I might do,
To right the wrong that she inferred,
And from my actions drew.

One course, and one alone I thought
Might make me innocent,
A copy of her book I bought.
A modest sum I spent.

A great investment it has been,
Advice both practical
And inspirational I've seen,
And none of it banal.

So now I beg forgiveness
For accidental wrong,
And ask that finally she bless
My penitential song.

Nola

You see those samplers, there upon the wall.
They were my wife's. Her needlework I think
Grew finer year by year, as did her soul.
She quite wore out the chair, all green and pink,
In which she sewed, and so I had to set it by,
Though not the couch, beneath the window there.
On which, when she was ill, she used to lie
To hear me read aloud. I cannot bear
To change it now.

Those pictures on the table by the door
I cherish for their record of her face
From wedding day to just a month before
She died, as beautiful and full of grace
As when, in San Francisco, on that day
We met, eyes locked across a crowded room,
And knew that we must take this offered way
To happiness, or live forever in a sad vacuum
Of might have beens.

That bible in the leather case was hers.
Often she read it through within a year,
And sometimes she would gently urge, and spur
Me to the same. I never did I fear.
There are three shelves of books that were her own,
Some Art, but most religious works.
I know that had she lived I might have grown
To love them, but, without her, I just shirk
The serious pursuit of faith.

That dog-eared score of Mozart's Requiem,
The last work that we sang together,
Reminds me of a happier time when,
In an LA bar, we so encouraged her,
She sang a song from some hit musical
With voice and manner of an ingenue.
She looked so young and beautiful, that all
The patrons were, like me, entranced and knew
That this was someone fine.

But gentlemen, I am your host,
You have not come to hear my memories
Of that dear one I loved the most,
But to discuss the music which might please
The guests at my next dinner party

Addendum

"Definitely" Random Quotes
The sources of the quotes are, in order: William Shakespeare, Robert Browning, John Keats, Lord Byron, Lord John Wilmot, Sir John Suckling, William Wordsworth, Samuel Taylor Coleridge, Sir Henry Newbolt, Thomas Gray, Edmund Spenser, Robert Herrick, A. E. Houseman, Lewis Carroll, William Shakespeare, Ralph Waldo Emerson, The Rubiayat of Omar Khyayam (Edward Fitzgerald), John Donne, William Blake, D. H. Lawrence.

Memorial Mall
Memorial Mall takes its name from the Memorial district in Houston, transected by Memorial Drive which, in addition, passes through Memorial Park. Memorial Drive was named in memory of the men who served in Camp Logan, which was a World War I-era army training camp, situated on the present site of Memorial Park.

On Tracey Emin Being Considered for the Turner Prize
The last two lines refer to Turner's famous quote;

"If I could find anything blacker than black, I'd use it."
                              -William Joseph Mallord Turner

Mourning Doves and Passenger Pigeons

The Passenger Pigeon, genus Ectopistes migratorius, is an extinct North American bird that lived in enormous migratory flocks until the early 20th century, when hunting and habitat destruction led to its demise. Mourning Doves are one of the most abundant and widespread of all North American birds, and are closely related to passenger Pigeons. They are both members of family Columbidae.

On Walking the SW Coast Path

The **South West Coast Path** is England's longest waymarked footpath. It stretches for 630 miles (1,014km), running from Minehead in Somerset, along the coasts of Devon and Cornwall, to Poole Harbour in Dorset. Since it rises and falls with every river mouth, it is also one of the more challenging trails. The total height climbed has been calculated to be 114,931ft (35,031m), almost four times the height of Mount Everest.

Thoughts on Visiting Hadrian's Wall

For any non-Texans, "our southern fence" refers to the fence being erected along the US border with Mexico.

Inspired by Galileo's Last Words

Eppur si muove (and still it moves) is an Italian phrase said to have been used by Galileo when he recanted his testimony before the Inquisition. He was referring to the Earth orbiting the Sun.

Illustration Glossary